Seasons

Winnifred Coe Verbica

WINEPRESS WP PUBLISHING

ISBN 1-57921-183-6
Library of Congress Catalog Card Number: 99-62940

God's majesty is exalted through poetic descriptions and photographs of ever-changing seasons. Each month contains daily Bible verses and a keepsake record of anniversaries, birthdays, and answered prayers, culminating in your own prayer journal.

"Sing unto God, sing praises to His name: extol Him that rideth upon the heavens by His name . . . and rejoice before Him." (Psalm 68:4)

The hills of San Jose, California, home to my family for four generations, reflect God's great love for man and nature. As the pages of seasons turn year by year, God etches His timeless grandeur in both countryside and creature.

Journey with me through every month and let your heart be blessed and your soul stirred to a closer walk with Our Creator, as you lift to Him the remembrance of those you love.

"But they that wait upon the Lord shall renew their strength; they shall mount up with wings as eagles; they shall run, and not be weary; and they shall walk, and not faint." (Isaiah 40:31)

January

In January's Winter chill
an icy crust has covered all the ponds,
reflecting foliage on the hill
while banks are flanked by trees and fern-green fronds.

Small, hungry hummingbirds descend
to taste the nectar's sweetness in the flower.
They dart and flit amidst the wind
to soar, propelled by hidden strength and power.

And hawks that claim the treetop tower
yet float, their feathered wings outstretched and free,
may soon enjoy the Winter's shower,
while ground squirrels frisk below with seeming glee.

Bare willow branches sweep the ground,
where leaves lie dampened from the Winter rain.
Gold mustard hides a treasure found
within its tiny seeds inside the grain.

For God has given earth a rest.
Yes, He who authored seasons' changes here
provides for every creature's best,
because He guides the earth that He holds dear.

8

January

Birthdays/Anniversaries	Answered Prayers

1.

_____ John 3:16

2.

_____ Proverbs 27:2

3.

_____ Matthew 5:3

4.

_____ Proverbs 6:23

5.

_____ Matthew 12:35

6.

_____ Luke 11:28

7.

_____ Revelation 5:12

8.

_____ Lamentations 3:26

9.

_____ Ephesians 6:17

10.

_____ Psalms 119:165

11.

_____ Isaiah 32:17

12.

_____ Ephesians 4:25

13.

_____ 1 John 5:11

14.

_____ 1 Peter 5:6

15.

_____ Proverbs 16:1

January

Birthdays/Anniversaries	Answered Prayers
16.	
	James 4:7
17.	
	Philippians 4:8
18.	
	Proverbs 15:4
19.	
	Matthew 4:4
20.	
	Proverbs 11:20
21.	
	Hebrews 5:9
22.	
	Job 36:11
23.	
	2 Corinthians 4:17–18
24.	
	John 8:12
25.	
	Psalm 119:1
26.	
	Proverbs 22:4
27.	
	Psalm 25:10
28.	
	1 Timothy 4:8
29.	
	Hebrews 4:12
30.	
	1 John 3:21
31.	
	Revelation 22:14

"And he shall be like a tree planted by the rivers of water, that bringeth forth his fruit in his season; his leaf also shall not wither; and whatsoever he doeth shall prosper." (Psalm 1:3)

February

Chilly, February breathes on canyon floor.
Brilliant light descends on emerald green.
Miles of vegetation shape the mountain's door.
Windswept, nature shines new, fresh, and clean.

Birds' and insects' chatter fills the air around;
storms now rage through February days.
Movement shows that life is teeming o'er the ground
where the cattle, elk, and black tail graze.

Snowy newborn lambs arrive to greet the year,
toddling slowly after ewes, unsure.
Shepherds, watchful for their flocks of sheep, stay near.
Everywhere the vale seems fresh and pure.

Winter breezes sweep the bright green mountain land;
life, in all its varied forms aware,
rests in God's protection by the unseen hand
of the wondrous gentle Shepherd's care.

February

Birthdays/Anniversaries	Answered Prayers
1.	
	Proverbs 3:5–6
2.	
	Proverbs 13:20
3.	
	Psalm 65:3
4.	
	Psalm 133:1
5.	
	Isaiah 55:8–9
6.	
	Ecclesiastes 7:1
7.	
	2 Corinthians 5:17
8.	
	Hebrews 10:17
9.	
	2 Corinthians 5:17
10.	
	Hebrews 10:17
11.	
	Zechariah 13:9
12.	
	John 15:12–13
13.	
	1 John 4:10
14.	
	Philippians 1:7
15.	
	Matthew 5:7

February

Birthdays/Anniversaries	Answered Prayers
16.	
	Psalm 34:15
17.	
	Jeremiah 32:39
18.	
	Galatians 5:22–23
19.	
	Ephesians 3:12
20.	
	Jeremiah 33:8
21.	
	2 Corinthians 13:11
22.	
	1 John 3:18–19
23.	
	Psalm 89:34
24.	
	Psalm 33:21
25.	
	Proverbs 12:20
26.	
	Galatians 6:9
27.	
	Matthew 5:16
28.	
	1 Corinthians 2:9–10
29.	
	Matthew 18:19–20

"For I know the thoughts that I think toward you, saith the Lord, thoughts of peace, and not of evil, to give you an expected end."
(Jeremiah 29:11)

March

*A*pple trees with blossoms on their boughs,
adorned in March's fine array,
glow like milk-white sturdy Charolais cows
that wander over hills today.

Fragrance from new roses on the vine
pervades the atmosphere with scent.
Crimson petals cling to stems like wine,
as nature seems to ponder Lent.

Leaves now bring the limbs their gift of Spring;
chartreuse new life emerges, bold.
March's glorious winds, resounding, sing
with secrets they cannot withhold!

Pure and holy Majesty assigns
such vibrant joy and hope to earth.
Apple trees and roses, God's designs,
remind the world of its great worth.

March

Birthdays/Anniversaries	Answered Prayers

1._____

_____ Proverbs 16:9

2._____

_____ Psalm 119:97

3._____

_____ Revelation 1:3

4._____

_____ 1 John 5:4

5._____

_____ Matthew 12:37

6._____

_____ Psalm 34:22

7._____

_____ John 16:24

8._____

_____ John 8:32

9._____

_____ Romans 8:6

10._____

_____ Psalm 112:1

11._____

_____ Philippians 4:7

12._____

_____ Psalm 5:12

13._____

_____ Isaiah 61:1

14._____

_____ John 5:28–29

15._____

_____ Romans 10:13–15

March

Birthdays/Anniversaries	Answered Prayers

16.	
	Acts 16:31
17.	
	Proverbs 11:18
18.	
	Colossians 1:15–16
19.	
	1 John 4:12
20.	
	Colossians 3:13
21.	
	Psalm 71:5
22.	
	Isaiah 40:8
23.	
	Psalm 32:8
24.	
	1 Peter 1:25
25.	
	Colossians 3:15
26.	
	Ezekiel 36:27
27.	
	Proverbs 16:18
28.	
	Psalm 37:18
29.	
	Romans 8:2
30.	
	Proverbs 16:3
31.	
	James 1:2–4

"Oh that men would praise the Lord for His Goodness, and for His wonderful works to the children of men! For He satisfieth the longing soul and filleth the hungry soul with goodness." (Psalm 107:8–9)

April

*A*pril: *noble time of blackbirds winging,*
their sounds resounding through the valley, bonny green.
Air shines crisp and filled with bird songs ringing,
while redwings soar and shimmer with a silver sheen.

April bursts with life as God had promised,
when seeds were sown in fertile soil so long ago.
Nature seems to sing as did the Psalmist,
"Let's make a joyful noise," while grain and seedlings grow!

Earth cannot contain its joy-filled sharing,
for rain has soaked the ground and sun has warmed the seeds.
Through all this, our Father shows His caring
and promises to separate the wheat from weeds.

Easter carries April's greatest treasure . . .
the cross, the grave, the resurrection through our Lord.
Faithfulness surpassing human measure
gives hope, as sprouting seeds present new life outpoured.

We may celebrate the joy of living,
absorbing songs the valley sends in sweetest prayer.
God, whose nature blessed us by His giving,
provides this panorama of His Love and care.

April

Birthdays/Anniversaries	Answered Prayers
1.	Psalm 34:17
2.	2 Timothy 4:8
3.	Psalm 23:6
4.	Luke 12:37
5.	John 1:29
6.	Luke 11:10
7.	2 Corinthians 4:1
8.	Romans 8:32
9.	Revelation 22:12
10.	Zechariah 12:10
11.	1 John 3:2
12.	Hebrews 10:36
13.	1 Corinthians 15:51–52
14.	Psalm 37:5
15.	Matthew 16:27

April

Birthdays/Anniversaries	Answered Prayers
16.	Proverbs 16:32
17.	Proverbs 3:31
18.	Romans 2:6–8
19.	Psalm 138:7
20.	Titus 3:4–5
21.	John 1:12
22.	Psalm 37:4
23.	2 Peter 3:3–4, 10
24.	Psalm 17:15
25.	John 14:13
26.	Mark 11:24
27.	John 14:2–3
28.	1 Peter 5:4
29.	Luke 22:29–30
30.	1 Corinthians 9:16

"Wait on the Lord: be of good courage, and He shall strengthen thine heart: wait, I say, on the Lord." (Psalm 27:14)

May

Violet blue and purple irises display the border;
roses burst with blossoms in full bloom.
Cotton-light, the fluffy clouds delight in snow-white order
while the fragrant zephyrs send perfume.

Warm and gentle breezes carry pine trees' yellowed pollen,
floating, dust-like through the Springtime air.
Cattle wade knee-deep across the mountain creek once swollen.
Hungry boar are rooting stream banks bare.

Caring deer give birth to fawns that nestle close together.
Tawny lions search to feed their cubs,
while the bobcat waits with fervent patience near the heather,
and the rodent scuttles from the shrubs.

Fragrant flowers beaming in the fields and gardens gaily
dance 'neath clouds that float across the sky.
All the meadow basks in awe of God's provision daily;
praises to the Lord of hosts draw nigh!

May

Birthdays/Anniversaries	Answered Prayers
1.	
	1 Peter 3:15
2.	
	Matthew 17:20
3.	
	Psalm 55:22
4.	
	Romans 8:18
5.	
	Psalm 34:18
6.	
	1 Corinthians 11:26
7.	
	Psalm 91:11
8.	
	Zechariah 4:6
9.	
	John 14:12
10.	
	Proverbs 16:23
11.	
	1 Corinthians 2:9–10
12.	
	Proverbs 12:4
13.	
	John 6:37–40
14.	
	Proverbs 31:10–12
15.	
	Proverbs 22:6

May

Birthdays/Anniversaries	Answered Prayers
16.	
	Philippians 2:12–13
17.	
	Romans 6:22–23
18.	
	Proverbs 15:15
19.	
	John 14:27
20.	
	Proverbs 3:25–26
21.	
	John 14:27
22.	
	1 Peter 5:5
23.	
	Isaiah 1:18
24.	
	Revelation 21:6
25.	
	Proverbs 18:10
26.	
	Ephesians 2:10
27.	
	Psalm 107:9
28.	
	1 Timothy 6:17
29.	
	Proverbs 5:19
30.	
	Colossians 3:13
31.	
	Isaiah 55:11

"Fear thou not; for I am with thee: be not dismayed; for I am thy God: I will strengthen thee; yea, I will help thee; yea, I will uphold thee with the right hand of my righteousness." (Isaiah 41:10)

June

June's parade of sun-drenched wonder welcomes me.
Delightful reddish-yellow marigolds
bloom in flower beds near forest-green oak tree.
Dry oats and vetch portray each golden fold
as all the fields of warmer days unfold.

Summertime with God's protective cloak and care
displays a day that's filled with butterflies.
White and bronze, they seem to close their wings in prayer.
The earthbound caterpillars as they die,
through God, become the butterflies that fly!

Waves of warmth provide the Summer day with calm,
and hummingbirds pursue their quest for food.
Aloe vera flowers share June's gladsome psalm,
as stamen's nectar feeds the bird it wooed:
a majesty of Summer's winsome mood!

June

Birthdays/Anniversaries	Answered Prayers
1.	
	Romans 1:16
2.	
	Proverbs 18:24
3.	
	John 17:3
4.	
	Galatians 3:14
5.	
	Romans 5:1
6.	
	John 20:20
7.	
	1 Thessalonians 4:16–17
8.	
	Psalm 119:105
9.	
	Joel 2:28
10.	
	1 Corinthians 2:12
11.	
	Psalm 33:18–19
12.	
	John 19:13
13.	
	Galatians 6:1
14.	
	Hebrews 10:38
15.	
	Proverbs 19:11

June

Birthdays/Anniversaries	Answered Prayers
16.	Psalm 126:5
17.	Psalm 91:1
18.	Romans 14:21
19.	2 Corinthians 3:17
20.	Colossians 1:27
21.	Psalm 37:40
22.	Matthew 24:30
23.	Philippians 1:29
24.	Romans 6:23
25.	2 Timothy 3:16
26.	Psalm 48:14
27.	1 John 2:1
28.	Proverbs 17:17
29.	1 Corinthians 12:13
30.	1 John 2:12

"For every beast of the forest is Mine, and the cattle upon a thousand hills." (Psalm 50:10)

July

Coyote's piercing cry resounds at dawn;
he stands a silhouette, alone.
A frightened doe secures her fragile fawn
that blends with tawny field in tone.

July presents damp warmth of Summer heat.
Wild turkeys cool themselves at noon
along creek banks where cattle lie replete
from grasses yellowed during June.

Yet God has etched His clouds throughout the sky
in bold tableau of Summertime.
The hawks descend to earth then lift and fly
to soar and circle as they climb.

Coyotes, turkeys, cattle, deer, and hawks
delight themselves in life today.
The Lord who shouts through all the hills and rocks
is wielding nature's grand display!

July

Birthdays/Anniversaries	Answered Prayers
1.	
	Isaiah 53:5
2.	
	Psalm 19:7–8
3.	
	Hebrews 9:22
4.	
	2 Chronicles 7:14
5.	
	Ephesians 2:8–9
6.	
	Hebrews 9:14
7.	
	Romans 5:8
8.	
	Romans 5:9
9.	
	Isaiah 40:11
10.	
	1 Peter 2:24
11.	
	Colossians 1:13–14
12.	
	Luke 10:27
13.	
	1 Timothy 6:7
14.	
	Hebrews 9:15
15.	
	Ephesians 2:13

July

Birthdays/Anniversaries	Answered Prayers
16.	
	Ephesians 1:7
17.	
	1 John 1:9
18.	
	1 John 1:7
19.	
	Ephesians 1:17
20.	
	1 Corinthians 14:33
21.	
	Proverbs 20:24
22.	
	Hebrews 13:8
23.	
	Matthew 26:28
24.	
	1 John 2:15
25.	
	Galatians 1:3
26.	
	Matthew 24:35
27.	
	Romans 5:6
28.	
	1 Peter 2:18–19
29.	
	Titus 2:11–12
30.	
	1 Peter 1:18–19
31.	
	Hebrews 6:12

"*Great is our Lord, and of great power: His understanding is infinite.*"
(*Psalm 147:5*)

August

August warmth caresses cattle
as Summer nears its close.
Blackbirds group prepared for battle,
near shrieking, stalking crows.

Pigeons cling to barns like roses
awaiting to be picked.
Bucks and does in fields touch noses,
their Summer sentry pricked!

August foals announce arrival
and toddle after mares.
Hills leave traces where survival
is marred by lions' lairs.

Gentle breezes touch the willows
to cradle each green leaf.
Calves use fodder as their pillows;
oh, Summertime is brief!

Waiting for the August blessing
are all the birds and deer.
God will never keep them guessing;
His Will is sovereign here.

August

Birthdays/Anniversaries

Answered Prayers

1.

2.

3.

4.

5.

6.

7.

8.

9.

10.

11.

12.

13.

14.

15.

Psalm 25:9

1 Corinthians 15:55–57

Isaiah 45:24

Proverbs 28:13

Galatians 6:8

Isaiah 42:9

Hebrews 11:1

Romans 8:38–39

Psalm 37:39

Hebrews 11:6

Matthew 18:19

Galatians 5:22–23

John 10:27–28

Psalm 95:6–7

Psalm 16:8

August

Birthdays/Anniversaries	Answered Prayers
16.	
	Matthew 5:6
17.	
	Romans 8:28
18.	
	Romans 8:11
19.	
	Psalm 55:17
20.	
	Revelation 3:20
21.	
	Romans 5:10–11
22.	
	John 14:23
23.	
	Joel 2:27
24.	
	John 15:15
25.	
	1 Thessalonians 4:14
26.	
	Psalm 4:3
27.	
	Matthew 28:20
28.	
	John 11:35
29.	
	Psalm 119:2
30.	
	John 15:5
31.	
	Romans 3:31

"Blessed is the man that trusteth in the Lord, and whose hope the Lord is." (Jeremiah 17:7)

September

September waits to shower lawns with leaves
as nature whispers gentle Autumn greeting.
Brown fields, now bare, lie void of Summer sheaves
while blue jays, blackbirds, pigeons swarm in meeting.

September brings the plough to break the ground,
and wildlife scurry to avoid the chopping.
Soft caterpillars crawl from mound to mound,
as cottontails resume their fervent hopping.

While furry squirrels chase from place to place,
their holes a maze of underground construction,
white, bay, and sorrel horses choose to race
upon the surface, watching each obstruction.

Could any doubt the order God has placed
upon the earth? No! Only a Creator
could give His creatures such a perfect taste
of Heaven! Only Heaven could be greater!

September

Birthdays/Anniversaries	Answered Prayers
1.	
	Deuteronomy 31:8
2.	
	Proverbs 10:25
3.	
	Psalm 55:22
4.	
	Deuteronomy 29:29
5.	
	Ephesians 4:31–32
6.	
	Psalm 84:11
7.	
	2 Corinthians 4:14
8.	
	John 6:58
9.	
	Romans 8:14
10.	
	1 Peter 3:1–2
11.	
	Acts 2:39
12.	
	1 Peter 13–14
13.	
	Ephesians 6:10–11
14.	
	John 5:24
15.	
	Philippians 1:6

September

Birthdays/Anniversaries	Answered Prayers
16._____	_____
_____	_Hebrews 10:26–27
17._____	_____
_____	_John 6:47
18._____	_____
_____	_Proverbs 8:17
19._____	_____
_____	_1 Peter 1:8–9
20._____	_____
_____	_Ephesians 4:14–15
21._____	_____
_____	_John 11:25
22._____	_____
_____	_Psalm 9:1
23._____	_____
_____	_2 Timothy 2:24–25
24._____	_____
_____	_2 Timothy 2:22
25._____	_____
_____	_Matthew 24:27
26._____	_____
_____	_Philippians 4:7
27._____	_____
_____	_Psalm 140:13
28._____	_____
_____	_Hebrews 2:18
29._____	_____
_____	_Lamentations 3:22–23
30._____	_____
_____	_2 Corinthians 3:5

"For ye shall go out with joy, and be led forth with peace: the mountains and the hills shall break forth before you into singing, and all the trees of the field shall clap their hands." (Isaiah 55:12)

October

*I*t's here: bright Autumn season of the year!
Redheaded woodpeckers attack tall pines.
Thin willows hold their leaves like secret tears.
The fiery sun with Autumn glory shines,
though from the West a subtle cloud appears.

Glad Autumn marigolds adorn the ground,
while fields once gold with buttercups and oats
lie paled, their furrowed faces wrinkled, frowned.
White oats hold fast to green and olive coats,
and "yellow jackets" buzz their warning sound.

October starts this grey-green time of Fall.
Light-bronze and golden leaves on paper birch
acclaim the mystery of Autumn's call.
They decorate the branches as a church.
Like steeples, birch trees stretch both free and tall.

And so with varied colors God proclaims
October's melodrama for His saints.
While squash and pumpkins shine like amber flames,
the mighty hand of God descends and paints
a world of beauty as the earth exclaims!

October

Birthdays/Anniversaries	Answered Prayers
1.	
	Ephesians 4:29
2.	
	Philippians 4:19
3.	
	John 15:11
4.	
	Acts 1:11
5.	
	Luke 12:32
6.	
	John 6:39
7.	
	Mark 16:17–18
8.	
	Luke 12:28
9.	
	2 Corinthians 12:9
10.	
	1 Corinthians 2:12
11.	
	Proverbs 28:26
12.	
	Psalm 91:2
13.	
	Psalm 27:1
14.	
	Revelation 22:5
15.	
	Matthew 6:19–21

October

Birthdays/Anniversaries	Answered Prayers
16.	Psalm 28:8
17.	Psalm 46:1
18.	Revelation 21:7
19.	Matthew 25:34
20.	Proverbs 1:5
21.	Romans 14:17
22.	James 5:15
23.	1 Peter 5:8–9
24.	Hebrews 11:16
25.	2 Peter 3:13
26.	Proverbs 22:1
27.	Mark 16:15
28.	1 John 4:1
29.	1 Timothy 4:1
30.	2 Corinthians 11:14
31.	Deuteronomy 18:10–12

". . . Holy, holy, holy, is the Lord of hosts: the whole earth is full of His glory." (Isaiah 6:3)

November

November dawns ablaze in glory,
for wind and rain have swept the land!
Brown sparrows share Thanksgiving's story
with turkeys wild, their feathers fanned.

Stark drama greets November morning.
New changes in the sky appear.
Dark clouds now whisper Winter's warning
with lively magpies prancing near.

Great oak trees ring with redwings' singing;
no breeze allows the leaves to blow.
Yet sun with newfound warmth is bringing
the strength for dormant seeds to grow.

Blue herons stretch in bright green fringes
of fields that yawn in valley's light.
The fog has left its dampened tinges
and grasses seem to shimmer white.

November's cache of creatures rally
and gratitude from earth resounds!
Throughout the broad expanse of valley
exuberance for God abounds.

November

Birthdays/Anniversaries	Answered Prayers

1._____

_____ 1 Corinthians 4:5

2._____

_____ John 16:33

3._____

_____ Psalm 23:1

4._____

_____ Revelation 1:7

5._____

_____ 2 Thessalonians 3:5

6._____

_____ Psalm 9:9

7._____

_____ Matthew 7:1–2

8._____

_____ Proverbs 28:5

9._____

_____ Hebrews 9:28

10._____

_____ 1 John 5:20

11._____

_____ 1 Samuel 2:9

12._____

_____ Proverbs 27:1

13._____

_____ Romans 15:5

14._____

_____ Isaiah 2:3

15._____

_____ John 14:18

November

Birthdays/Anniversaries	Answered Prayers
16.	
	Proverbs 9:10
17.	
	Revelation 7:16–17
18.	
	James 4:8
19.	
	Psalm 1:1
20.	
	2 Timothy 2:12
21.	
	Philippians 1:7
22.	
	Psalm 94:14
23.	
	John 1:16–17
24.	
	2 Corinthians 4:8–9
25.	
	Psalm 27:10
26.	
	Galatians 6:7–8
27.	
	Psalm 40:1
28.	
	Matthew 5:10
29.	
	Ecclesiastes 7:8
30.	
	Hebrews 4:16

"Peace I leave with you, My peace I give unto you: not as the world giveth, give I unto you. Let not your heart be troubled, neither let it be afraid." (John 14:27)

December

Sparrows greet the season in December sun
and peck at tasty morsels on the ground.
Frisky does and fawns enjoy a Winter run
amid the oak trees' acorns they have found.

Bulky Hereford cattle graze on sloping knoll
near feed troughs filled as mangers long ago.
Christmas stirs the heart of every ransomed soul
who chooses truth and humbly seeks to grow.

Trees and birds and animals reflect God's joy
in sharing Heaven's treasures here below,
for the Savior came to earth a baby boy
who in the stable heard the cattle low.

God considers even sparrows great in worth,
and every part of water, earth, and sky.
Yes, He sent His Son in such a lowly birth
that every child of His might live on high.

Hope abides as life and nature celebrate
this perfect gift from God the Father's hand.
Christmas light and love beside the manger state
the blessed gift of peace throughout the land.

December

Birthdays/Anniversaries	Answered Prayers
1.	Psalm 32:1
2.	Isaiah 55:7
3.	Romans 12:21
4.	Colossians 3:4
5.	Isaiah 35:8
6.	Matthew 1:20–21
7.	Psalm 127:3
8.	Hebrew 10:22
9.	Matthew 3:3
10.	Proverbs 12:19
11.	Matthew 24:42
12.	Isaiah 42:16
13.	1 Corinthians 15:9
14.	1 Peter 5:5
15.	1 Timothy 6:6

December

Birthdays/Anniversaries	Answered Prayers
16.	
	Psalm 103:2–3
17.	
	Isaiah 41:10
18.	
	Proverbs 10:32
19.	
	Hebrews 10:23
20.	
	Psalm 64:10
21.	
	Romans 8:37
22.	
	John 16:33
23.	
	Hebrews 8:12
24.	
	1 Thessalonians 5:23
25.	
	John 1:1, 14
26.	
	Psalm 85:8
27.	
	Job 19:25
28.	
	1 Corinthians 13:4–6, 8
29.	
	Revelation 2:10
30.	
	Jeremiah 31:34
31.	
	Revelation 21:4

"Thou wilt show me the path of life: in Thy presence is fulness of joy; at Thy right hand there are pleasures for evermore." (Psalm 16:11)

Personal Prayer Journal

"For now we see through a glass darkly; but then face to face: now I know in part; but then shall I know even as also I am known." (I Corinthians 13:12)

Personal Prayer Journal

*"Oh, the depth of the riches both of the wisdom and knowledge of God!
How unsearchable are His judgments, and His ways past finding out."
(Romans 11:33)*

Personal Prayer Journal

"*. . . I am the way, the truth, and the life: no man cometh unto the Father, but by Me.*" *(John 14: 6)*

Personal Prayer Journal

"For we know that if our earthly house of this tabernacle were dissolved, we have a building of God, an house not made with hands, eternal in the heavens." (II Corinthians 5:1)

This book is dedicated to family and friends who have encouraged me through the years. It is a special tribute to my father, Henry Sutcliffe Coe, who instilled in me a love for the land, and to my husband, Robert George Verbica, who has shared this love. The photographs were taken as Bob and I spent time together in these California hills. Part of the ranch is now Henry Coe State Park, given as a tribute to my grandfather by my aunt, Sada Coe Robinson.

I will lift up mine eyes unto the hills, from whence cometh my help. My help cometh from the Lord, which made heaven and earth. (Psalm 121:1–2)

To order additional copies of

Seasons

send $11.95 plus shipping and handling to

Books Etc.
PO Box 4888
Seattle, WA 98104

or have your credit card ready and call

(800) 917-BOOK